BE THE MOUNTAIN

Life Lessons Taught By Nature

Be Your Best you ---
Be the Mountain!
Cheri Kretsch

Copyright © 2017, 2018 Cheri A. Kretsch
Published by Natural Lessons, LLC.

All rights reserved. No part of this publication may be reproduced, distributed, or transmitted in any form or by any means, including photocopying, recording, or other electronic or mechanical methods, without the prior written permission of the publisher, except in the case of brief quotations embodied in critical reviews and certain other noncommercial uses permitted by copyright law.

Be the Mountain
By Cheri Henke Kretsch

Publisher's Cataloging-In-Publication Data
(Prepared by The Donohue Group, Inc.)

Names: Kretsch, Cheri Henke, author.
Title: Be the Mountain / Cheri Henke Kretsch.
Description: [Second edition]. | [Littleton, Colorado] : Natural Lessons, LLC, [2018] | Series: Life lessons taught by nature ; [book 1]
Identifiers: ISBN 9781732913509 | ISBN 9781732913516 (ebook)
Subjects: LCSH: Mountains--Psychological aspects. | Mountains--Poetry. | Mountains--Pictorial works. | Conduct of life. | Self-actualization (Psychology) | Self-esteem.
Classification: LCC BF353.5.N37 K74 2018 (print) | LCC BF353.5.N37 (ebook) | DDC 155.91--dc23

Library of Congress Control Number: 2018913300

First published in 2017 by Cheri A. Kretsch

www.natural-lessons.com

BE THE MOUNTAIN

Life Lessons Taught By Nature

CHERI HENKE KRETSCH

EARTH'S LESSONS

We are all mountains
      strength at its peak
      potential is endless
      challenge we seek.

We are all valleys
      with bruises so deep
      to be at the bottom
      through climbing we weep.

We are all rocks
      secure as a whole
      the pile then crumbles
      new places to go.

We are all grasses
      moving with ease
      a swaying contentment
      it's all such a breeze.

I am with nature
      for as long as I please
      I thank you, Mother Earth,
      for the lessons about me.

CONTENTS

The Story Begins	1
Chapter 1: Frustration, Irritability, and Anger	12
Chapter 2: Hope and Perseverance	20
Chapter 3: Flexibility and Change	26
Chapter 4: Courageously Brave	36
Chapter 5: Balance Created in Contrast & Opposites	46
Chapter 6: Unique yet Stable	54
Chapter 7: Respect All Things	60
Chapter 8: Success	68
Chapter 9: Be Quiet—Be Still	76
Chapter 10: Dreams and the Big Picture	82
Chapter 11: Be Uplifting	90
Acknowledgments	98
About the Author	102

A PLACE FOR NATURE

A simple joy upon the rocks
A breathtaking view to behold.
    Inhaling the solemn contentment
    While studying its beauty at length…

        I sense its rarity and strength.

The snow glistens from distant mountains
The raging rivers at their feet
    The balance without flaws
    All geometrically in place…

        I sense its perfection and grace.

The little critters bustle all day
The hummingbirds zip by
    I listen to the perfect choir
    As I relax and sigh…

        The simple joys money can't buy.

THE STORY BEGINS

NATURE AS MY TEACHER

I was raised as a Colorado mountain girl. This, in part, would explain my love for nature as well as the development of my greatest coping skill. Not only was I taught to respect all life, but I was deeply appreciative of all that nature gave to me. Nature was my grounding, my solace, and my deepest love. I have always had the ability to see nature as a living, breathing soul. So it was easy to relate my human experiences to her. She could show me how a tiny, delicate flower could break a stone in half or how the weather could bring a rainbow after its harshest rains or how a devastating fire from lightning could refresh the forest as a beautiful basket of wildflowers. Nature seemed to have rhyme and reason when humans let me down.

In a nutshell (a few highlighted here), as a child, I experienced being (literally) blown up by dynamite with the death of my father (he was thirty five) at age ten; went through physical, emotional, and sexual abuses through family members and stepfathers; was date-raped in college; and lost my brother to a rattlesnake bite (he was only thirty-four). By the age of thirty-five, I had already lost so many of my family and friends that I felt I was a jinx. Adding to these losses was my disillusionment over what it meant to be loved. I learned to trust only me. In my survival mind, I was on my own. I won't go into all the details of discussing the wounds! Everybody is wounded in one way or another. My intent is to show how we grow through them, if we so choose. What is most important is how it defined me, how it shaped my life, and how it made me into the person I am proud to be. I'm hoping that at some point in our lives, we can all be proud of who we have become. My scars are to be honored, but they don't define me. I am greater than any event in my life—if I choose to learn and grow from it.

From early on, after my father died, I had a deep fire inside me. That fire would come out in the harshest times, saying, "No one, or no event, will take me down—I'm a good person." I'd sit and cry in nature like she was my confidant. Our dog Smokey got an earful, too. I'd sit for hours, writing poem after poem, trying to explain my feelings. So between the three, I survived childhood and my teen years. Somehow I just knew that one day I'd be free—free from the adults and their choices. One day, I'd be on my own. That sense of freedom, the love of nature and animals, with the ability to write poetry, is what carried me through the difficult times (and still does today). Nature made sense, the family dog seemed to love me unconditionally, and writing allowed me a space to share my feelings.

One of my most vivid memories as a child was when my father died. I stood at his coffin, patting it, and said "It's okay, Dad, I'll take care of Mom." Not sure where this responsible child arose from, but there she was! So at ten years old, I became responsible for everyone's happiness, not just my mom's. I felt responsible for my family's happiness as well as friends, strangers, and to the world of misfortunes. So, of course, in college, I majored in psychology and sociology. Go figure, right? I really needed to understand human beings. The more I understood, the more helpful I could be. I felt that by helping others, I could make sense out of my own pain. The pain in my heart was from not being able to believe what people said or did. The unconscious coping skill that I developed was my ability to override my heart, my sadness, my disillusionment . . . my feelings. When my heart would tell me one thing and my head another, the head won. I always felt deep compassion for others—I just couldn't do it for myself. Humans and their life events became a puzzle to be solved. Do we really mean what we say, and if so, why would we say that? Or why do we say one thing and do another? Or why are we the only animals that intentionally hurt others? Why are we dishonest for self-gain? There were so many questions that didn't make any sense to me. I wanted facts—I no longer would trust my feelings.

Nature made sense to me. I could count on her stability. After a destruction, she'd make things new, unique, and beautiful. I'd look to the mountains, rainbows, wildflowers, or the flowing waters to give me calm—to bring me peace. Nature provided some form of predictability. Out of chaos and destruction, I could see that the phoenix would rise. I could relate to this; it seemed like the theme in my life. I could relate to its suffering and overcoming. I was determined not to be a victim to my circumstances. I would be better than that. I was going to be stronger, wiser, and learn to love life—regardless of what it threw at me. I became the warrior for special human causes or anyone who needed someone to fight for him/her to right a wrong.

The fortunate part of my story is that people I never expected were the people who stepped into my life in a crisis and helped. Because of their generosity of caring, I, too, learned to care genuinely. I can now look back and feel proud and hopeful that I've helped others on their personal journeys as well. I'm grateful for following my warrior instincts. As I've learned from others, there were so many other ways I could have gone.

Through my professions and passions, I've been allowed to work with handicapped children as a teacher and become a licensed psychotherapist working in the high schools, private practice, and for government and on military bases. I have done presentations to hundreds, taught personal-empowerment courses, and was an adjunct professor in psychology. I have been fortunate to have had so many incredible experiences and met so many wonderful people along my journey. I have been empowered by people whom I have loved and respected. I have learned that there are great people out there who would love you and stand by your side. With trust being difficult for me, genuinely letting people in was a huge feat. To this day, I have many long-term, loving relationships that are deeply cherished. It's a feeling of deep appreciation and gratitude—a love that's far deeper than anything I can describe.

Even with loving people in my life, I could not have gotten to that genuine place without the love of nature. She showed me that it's okay to get hurt and pick yourself back up and keep going. She opened the door to possibilities. She showed me that there are rewards along the way—if I choose to see them. Those rewards are based in hope, growth, caring, and wisdom. I developed a sense of wonder in the human spirit and what it's capable of. As a psychotherapist with an expertise in trauma, I was constantly amazed at human resiliency. I was also aware of the diversity of pain and suffering and the problem-solving capabilities people could come up with in their survival scenarios. Each person, in his or her own unique way, showed courage and bravery. Through all this, I truly learned to honor and respect all living things, and I am grateful for that ability.

The greatest gift nature gave me, among the thousands, is that the sun will set on a crummy day, and the sun will rise, giving hope that it will be a better day. Most importantly, it's consistent—giving stability and security. Every day of my life, the sun has set, and the sun has risen the next day. I will be forever grateful for the reminder that life goes on. There is always hope. Now, every time the sun rises, I feel joy and respect in my heart. It warms my soul—every single day!

Nobody's journey, including my own, has been easy. It's a courageous development of love for self and others. My automatic survival coping skills gave way through knowledge of the harmful versus the helpful coping skills. With that in my toolbox, I learned to honor the emotional and psychological processes of time and the personal journey called life. Each person's journey is preciously unique. The greatest gift that I could give back was to first feel the gratefulness of my own journey. Then I could help empower and encourage others to have strength in their own abilities so they, too, could show their world how to be courageous and kind.

I wrote this first book, *Be the Mountain*, because the mountains gave me strength, showed me how to be unique and how to stand tall at all costs. They are the core of my being. For that reason, I started with the mountains. In the future, I hope to write about other elements of nature and their connectedness to our human experience. Every element of nature has special meaning and value to me. I hope you enjoy the journey.

PERSPECTIVE THROUGH EXPERIENCE

All my experiences, all my feelings toward those experiences, all my thoughts about them, and all the beliefs I derived from them have determined how I see life. All the knowledge I gained helped put things in perspective. Wisdom comes from both knowledge and experiences. I feel fortunate to have had *all* the experiences—the good and the hard.

One thing I've learned over the years is that no one can make you understand or see something that you're not ready for. I have developed a great respect for age and depth of character. I now get that it takes many years to be able to look back and understand the whole picture. I can see themes in my life and how they've played an important part of creating my being. I've learned that you can see something for the first time or the fiftieth time, but when you connect to it, it's the right time.

So often while growing up, I took my "not knowing something when someone else did" as not being smart enough or in-touch enough. What I have found is that there is something much greater than putting myself down. I now realize that I'm supposed to know what I know, when I know it. As for someone else's personal journey, he or she may have needed that information sooner than I did. Perhaps he or she needed it to build on its depth and complexity in order to fulfill it at the time it was needed. The true facts are that others are going to know more than you in some areas, while you'll know more than they will in other areas. Sometimes you'll have an idea about what the others are talking about—but at different levels of understanding. And sometimes you share a bond with others because you connect both with the right "theme" of information and the depth of the information. Those are special connections. You feel them right away. You sense your intrigue about them and how the two of you are alike thinkers and/or feelers. We will get some of them along our paths, but generally not many. It's the feeling that you get, yea or nay, that helps you to know whom to be connected to. The *nays* are just as powerful as the *yeas*, so pay attention to what your gut is telling you.

This is why we need to understand that no one is right or wrong. It's all about timing, understanding, and respecting each person's personal journey. It's our own perception and judgment that creates our unique journey. We're not here to challenge others' paths along their journeys. It's up to you to see if your path is a part of theirs or not. Do you connect—do you not? Do you enjoy a brief relationship on this path, a longer relationship as a journey, or not at all? Along our way we will find the things that are to make us grow—some pleasant, some not. All should be respected for what they have brought or are bringing to you. So if I can learn to respect your point of view (that does not mean I have to agree) and honor your own personal journey, then I no longer have a reason to be upset or in conflict with you. You are who you are. You are learning what you need to learn, at the time you're supposed to learn it, in the way you're supposed to receive it. I am the same. We are all trying to understand our human side and our deeper, spiritual side. The two are so different that it makes our lives conflicting. In trying to find a way to balance and synthesize it, we grow deeply. Come grow with me. Learn to master the human self so that your beautiful spirit can soar.

While knowing our experiences will be different, my hope is that you will find your own meaning and value in this book. So enjoy the journey through understanding the human experiences through the majesty of our mountains.

LET ME DANCE IN THE POWER

Seeing the majestic mountains
Gave me hope and courage;
Seeing the colorful wildflowers
Gave me the sense of freedom and change.

          I'll try to
          like the
    strength of the mountains;
          I'll try to
          accept the
    change of the wildflowers.

Spirit, give me the memories
Of mountains and wildflowers,

         Then let me
       Dance in the power
of my ever-changing, amazing strengths!

Photo Location: "Going to the Sun" Highway from Glacier National Park, Montana to Waterton, Canada

OH, THE *HURT*

I HURT…
    My tears bear the drizzling rains
    as a continuing melancholy sameness.

I HURT…
    My mind bears the ravishing floods
    seeking the space to everywhere.

I HURT…
    My body bears the deep, trembling earthquakes,
    accepting unknown time and upheaval.

I HURT…
    My heart bears the eruption of the volcano,
    covering all in my path with unexpected heat.

But while the earth hurts
    it begins anew
    filling the pain with growth.
If the mighty earth
    with its devastating pains
    can HEAL

    Then I can, too.

CHAPTER 1

FRUSTRATION, IRRITABILITY, AND ANGER

MOUNTAINS SHOW US FRUSTRATION, IRRITABILITY, AND ANGER

If you've ever watched a volcano, you'll understand how the mountain releases pent-up emotions. We're not exempt from difficult emotions. We all have them. It's what we do with them that matters.

The mountain shows its frustrations through steam and rumbling. It says, "You should pay attention." We're the same way. We blow off steam through yelling, kicking a chair, getting sick, or having a nervous stomach. It is the warning sign that more is about to happen, if you don't settle it down—*now!* The physical feeling is quite amazing! It starts in the gut area. You can feel its tenseness or its rumblings. As things progress, you can feel it rise all the way to your head! Angry energy always rises! By the time it reaches the upper chest/throat area, you will lose logical control, the ability to calm it down or walk away. It becomes a beast of emotion. Then whatever will happen *will* happen through intense emotion. It's at this point that you hear of people pulling out the gun or beating someone to death. It's in that instance of a second, having no logical control, that they created a horrible act. Most have no idea how it got there. The constricted blood flow to the brain shut down all cognitive stop signs. The moments became blurred in heated emotion. There are many prisoners who could tell you that they're not sure how it happened—sort of a blanking out. They didn't mean for it to get out of hand; it just did. What we need to understand is that our frustrations or irritabilities will automatically go down the path to anger. There is no other place for them to go unless you stay in your conscious, logical brain. We have to intercept the destructive energy before it gets to the upper chest area, or just like the volcano, it'll steam, rumble, and then spurt out some lava.

At some point the mountain is done warning, and the true spewing of lava bursts high into the air, lava seeping everywhere. Take note: everything the lava touches . . . dies. So, too, with angry humans—they spew from their mouths everything that *shouldn't* be said. They hurt people with their words and then their actions. The lava they spew won't allow for something better to grow. The damage, if repairable at all, will last for years before something better takes its place. The person that they were interacting with will always have a wary eye. No matter how bad the exploder feels, once the lava flows, it's sealed. You can't have the expectation of having that trusting relationship again. Though the relationship still may exist—it will be changed forever. The sad thing is that it only takes once. It's interesting that people may not remember what they were fighting about, but they'll never forget a name they were called. The insuring thoughts thereafter will be "*When* will he/she do it again?" Not *if*, but *when*. The damage is permanent on some level. Ask yourself: is this worth it? If I destroy all my relationships, how will I receive love? Learn to fight fair. Stay in your head; listen, don't assume; no name-calling; get control of yourself—cool down, put your brain into problem-solving mode.

I'm not talking about the abused or mentally ill here—that's a whole different issue. I'm talking about everyday people who have everyday stress to complicate their lives. We get upset about so many things that are out of our control. We want to have our spouses listen, to receive better service, or to encounter better drivers. It's not getting the salad we were looking forward to at lunch, or getting put down, or not getting something right. It's seldom the big stuff that gets to us. We can usually muster up the strength to get through a hard time. It's the everyday little stuff that takes us down. It's usually the buildup before that little thing boils over. So when we want things to get better, we'll have to start with the little stuff. We need to show our brain that it's capable of calming us down. Granted, there are many types of anger based on intensity and theme. The responses can range from rolling your eyes, to flipping someone off, to pulling out a gun. Only you can stop it before it gets out of hand.

If you say you can't control your anger, then I'm telling you that you're getting too much out of it. Maybe you like the surge of adrenalin, the power over someone, or you enjoy feeling the control through intimidation. Maybe you just want the passionate make-up sex after a good fight. The sad thing here is that you're hurting everyone else that's involved because of your twisted enjoyment. If you really don't want to destroy your relationships, then change your sense of self-responsibility. Take control over yourself.

First, figure out where your anger is at—physically. Then intervene by walking away or neutralizing it. That's why therapists suggest to "just walk away—cool down—get your head on straight." To neutralize it, start with self-talk. It would sound something like this: "If this person is bringing out the worst in me, should I still be in the relationship? Is this really how I want to expend my energy when I only get a limited amount of it? Is this worth going to jail over? Is this worth ruining my whole life? Is this worth dying over?" If we stay in the emotion, there is no way to harness it. We are all capable of destroying others—never underestimate your power under duress. Staying in the conscious mind allows us to maintain a focus and then find a solution.

I truly believe that ordinary anger is manageable. Get educated about your anger. Learn ways to deal with it. Pay attention to what you're getting from it. Watch a movie on volcanos and apply it to how your anger affects others. Remember that anger is a trait to be mastered. It won't happen overnight, but with each successful practice, you will control and limit the destruction. There's a reason we have volcanoes: to remind us of destruction. If we don't heed the warnings, the consequences are devastating and long term. Choose to be the dormant volcano—be the calm for you and others.

Be The Mountain—Heed Your Inner Rumblings.

.

INSIGHTS TO PONDER

1. Watch a movie on volcanoes—something on Hawaii or *National Geographic* specials.
   - Watch and hear people's reactions to it.
   - Watch the faces of those on whom you've unleashed your anger. Compare.
   - Compare the molten lava with your words. Notice anything?

2. Think about the last time you were frustrated, irritable, or angry.
   - How did it feel emotionally?
   - How about physically?
   - Promise yourself to become internally aware the next time it happens.

3. What or who brings out these feelings most often?
   - Do comments make you feel inadequate, embarrassed, or ashamed?
   - Do you feel disrespected, humiliated, or not heard?
   - Do events trigger you? Holidays, vacations, or family get-togethers.
   - Are you tired, stressed, depressed, or overanxious?
   - Again, pay attention—then start problem-solving.

4. How do you want to start responding in the future?
   - Think of past times you wish you would have reacted differently.
   - Replay them in your head—go back to #2 and ask those questions.
   - Try different ways of responding.
   - Find one that works for you and replay it in your head again and again and again until it feels comfortable (in your head). You want your brain to be familiar with what you want it to do—so it can help you when the anger happens again.

5. Thoughts to ponder:
   - If you want to "defend yourself," stop right there! If you believe that others are making judgments or assumptions about you that are wrong—then say nothing! You don't need to justify yourself to anyone. You know you! They don't! Give a look of caring indifference—then walk away. If you need to say something, try this: "You have the right to your own opinion." Do not qualify it further. Or look them in the eyes and say, "Wow! You obviously don't know me!" Let it go and walk away.
   - A person who knows him or herself can remain calm and content in or out of conflict.
   - Know what gets you going; then work on it to become indifferent to it.

GIVE ME...

Give me strength
    when I'm so empty
Give me freedom
    when my mind's tied down
Give me courage
    when I'm afraid
Give me hope
    when I'm so unsure
Give me joy
    when I'm unhappy
Give me peace
    when I'm confused
Give me faith
    when I'm questioning
Give me love
    when I'm all alone

CHAPTER 2

HOPE AND PERSEVERANCE

MOUNTAINS SHOW US HOPE AND PERSEVERANCE

If you've ever read about the pioneers crossing the mountains, you'll know how frustrated and fearful they were. The mountain was an obstacle to get through or around. The mountain wasn't going to move. They had to find their way through it. This required perseverance and a belief that it would get better soon. Perseverance means to continue doing something in spite of difficulty, to deal with opposition. The pioneers never knew what obstacles they would encounter in those mountains, but they kept the hope that they could get through it and live the dreams they had.

At the same time that the mountains also provided for them at the same time that it made things difficult. It provided water, shade, breezes, and beauty. It also gave them perspective as to where they were—they could see for miles. When the pioneers could be grateful for what the mountain provided, it just made it a little easier to get through it. If we can look and find gratefulness in our difficult journey, we, too, will find the hope to persevere. There is *always* good happening at the same time that the difficult is happening. It's not finding the good within the difficulty—it's finding it outside the difficulty. Just finding good in general will be helpful. We *automatically* focus on the difficulty—not by choice but by subconscious overprotection. So force yourself to see what good is also happening. It will allow your brain to perceive the difficulty . . . differently. As you have to get through this problem anyway, why not choose to get through it by seeing other good things happening to or for you? It truly eases the burden.

Perseverance doesn't mean that the difficulty will get immediately better or easier; what it means is that *you* have the ability to overcome the difficulty, one way or another. It is a challenge—physically, mentally, or emotionally.

Hope, on the other hand, is a belief. It's the vehicle to create the facts. If my fear base is the main driver, my brain will only be able to see other situations or scenarios that could possibly create more fearful situations. As I climb a mountain, if I look ahead and see the path is really steep, my brain has to create the fear that I won't make it. If I can redirect my brain and tell myself, "I've made it before; remember when you climbed Mount Sherman? That was no piece of cake, either, but you did it, and you were happy about it," then I can change my perception. My brain now can look ahead on the path and tell me to "just take one step at a time (like you've done before), and next thing you know, you'll be over that steep part." A new thought will give my brain permission to change its perceptions. It will not do it on its own. So be strong—be courageous. Tell your brain that you want to see something good or remember something good. Then it will create that for you.

If you think back . . . how many times could you have given up but didn't? It's the failed test, the lost love, the car accident that hurt you physically. Just like the mountains—there is always unpredictability! With every rock that falls or a creek that tears at its banks, or the lightning that changes forests, there is no set time or place—no predictability. We have to learn to count on our ability to adjust quickly . . . because we do and because we can! We need to figure out the tools that work for each of us that help us move along. The more flexible to change you are, the better you'll survive. The more prepared you are going into a new job, or a new relationship, a new financial opportunity, the better off you'll be to decide what's best for you. Beyond that whatever will happen will happen, so take your life toolbox with you—you'll always need it.

Beyond preparing as best you can, taking the learning tools that work best for you, and develop the ability of perseverance and hope. If it's something you believe in, keep putting one foot in front of the other. If it's based in your belief that it can and will get better, then your hopefulness will get you to the other side. Hope is the belief you need in the toolbox. Perseverance is the action to create the fulfillment of your dreams.

The Mountain Is The Obstacle. You Are The Power.
Persevere With Hopefulness.

INSIGHTS TO PONDER

1. Look at your mountains—your hardships. How have you endured?
   - How did you get through it or around it?
   - How did you know what to do or try?
   - What abilities did you use to overcome these difficulties?

2. Is there a theme in how you overcome difficulties?
   - Write down several situations that were difficult.
   - What thought helped you through? Has it helped you on more than one occasion?
   - How did you know where or when to apply it?
   - Do you have confidence in this ability to help you again?

3. While your mountains were presenting themselves, what good things were happening at the same time?
   - What kept you going forward?
   - What was your hope in getting through?
   - Looking back, would you have done it differently? If so, what do you wish you'd have done?
   - Using that replay, how would it have turned out?
   - How would that be beneficial to you now versus what it was? How would you be different today?

MOMENTS OF INSIGHT

There was a time
    for laughter and play;
Enjoying my family
    was all part of a day.

There was a time
    for questions and talk,
a deep conversation
    with friends I would walk.

There was a time
    for appreciative thoughts,
A beckoning silence,
    my stomach in knots.

There was a time
    when all was right,
when time was replaced
    with a moment of insight.

CHAPTER 3

FLEXIBILITY AND CHANGE

THE MOUNTAINS TEACH US FLEXIBILITY AND CHANGE

We, who live in Colorado, often look to our majestic mountains for many reasons. We see beauty . . . We see ruggedness . . . We see complexity and balance. But witnessing it and living in it are two totally different situations. If you've ever lived in the mountains, you know there is nothing simple about its survival. It's the snows that need to be plowed away, the rains that wash out a road or a bridge, the fire that shoots up a ravine, or the lava flowing down, removing everything in its path. For those who choose to live this way, it becomes a lesson in flexibility and change. They must learn to adjust to unforseen mishaps.

Mother Nature has her own agenda that we're not privy to. She will create hardships and devastations. But although it's difficult in the moment to see past the devastation, time heals the pains, and new life, new growth can occur. It will never be the same (in our lifetime)—it is, once again, new. After seeing the destruction of a fire, I was amazed at how many new things came forth. The wildflowers and grasses abounded, a little spring showed its bubbling head (never even knowing it had been there all along), and the new rock outcroppings (which I'd never seen before) were now majestic formations.

The same is true for us as human beings. When we experience hardship or devastation, we learn to adjust. We hurt for a while; we feel the pains that only we can feel. Our painful depth to that person or event is always unique. No one can feel it like you do, and no one can heal it except you. We feel the pain of our hearts breaking just as the mountain feels its devastating scars. None of it is easy—it is what it is. It is out of our control. Just like you can't stop someone from dying or becoming ill or having an accident, neither can the mountain stop Mother Nature's agenda. We can work with it, but we cannot control it. Yet we can learn from the mountains. We learn that to live means we will suffer—but we will also rise again in beauty and wisdom. I can choose to see the devastation and stay in sadness and remorse, or I can see what the newness will bring. It is totally up to me as an individual to see the options:

I can blame and complain—be victimized.

I can be aware that there's nothing I can do about it—so just feel the feelings and let time heal it.

I can stand in a neutral place, just being open to new hopes for something at least as good (though different).

I can believe that something better will take its place if I'm open enough to allow it to be what it needs to be, *now*, rather than what it was.

Understanding creates new thoughts. Yet understanding alone will not take away all the pains. We need to replace the old thoughts with something new—something we can build on—something hopeful, as we deal with the feelings of loss. Feeling the loss is important to do; you may feel anger, frustration, guilt, sadness, depression, or just plain being numb and overwhelmed. If you pay attention, at some point, you get tired of feeling down. You will want to make a change, just so you can feel a little better. This is that critical point of choosing to be a victim or finding hope and choosing to see things with a new understanding. There isn't a time factor to how fast or how slow someone should get through something. It's a very personal thing. If you pay attention to your gut, it'll tell you when enough is enough. Try not to override it through intellectualizing.

I've always told my clients, "If you are having a constant thought (obsessing), or it's stopping you from finding fun and joy in your life, then your mind is making the difficulty a habit. That's the time to start rebuilding." Start rebuilding the new, different you. You can never be that "old you" again. You have new information that you cannot pretend to not know or feel. You have a new experience under your belt with a whole load of new thoughts, feelings, and abilities to go with it. Take your new knowledge and feelings and ask yourself, "Who am I *now*?" Then create the *you* that you believe you are or wish to be. How do you want your future to look? How do you want to feel about those people or issues, *now*? What does the word "survivor" mean to you? Did you just get through, or are you a warrior spirit?

Here's an example of how a new creation might look. Let's say someone you loved has died. Find one endearing trait that made him or her special to you. Then practice being more of that trait. I call it the living memorial. There is no greater compliment or honor to our loved ones than to want to be more like their cherished character traits.

We need to learn how to hold ourselves to our higher standard. Notice the mountains. They stand tall. Through all their hardships, they remain powerful, strong, and always something to look up to. It's not what others think about how you should handle yourself after a hardship occurs—it's what *you* think about *you*! Our greatest gifts are our challenges; we learn more about ourselves and our capabilities. Do you see life as a challenge to find out more about you, or do you see it as a victim where everything happens to you—having no control?

The victim cries foul and wants to find blame and justification for his or her hurting. "If I hurt, then you should, too." Or "If I hurt, then you must have had it easier than me—you're lucky—I'm not." Or "If you didn't lose as much as I did, then you should feel bad for me." A victimized person can negatively suck in anyone around him/her—particularly empathetic people. If you are empathetic, you will feel the need to help compensate for that person's loss in physical, emotional, or economic ways. Do *not* participate in such unhealthy draining of your positivity and willing ability to help. Such people do not want your help; they want to drain you of all your goodness—and believe me, you will feel drained. I call them the "emotional vampires" of the universe. If you decide to work with them, protect yourself with strong boundaries. The victim accumulates, with honor, one misfortune after another—always assuming he or she has it worse than everyone else. The victim needs your sympathy and your energy so he or she won't feel so powerless and insecure. The sad part is that the victim can't see the good that can come from the hardship. Victims cannot see the goodness in their lives—period.

The people who can survive devastations are the ones that look to the future and decide it's a tragedy, but it won't stop them from living. They don't get stuck in the past and wallow or obsess—they allow the future to bring new hope, new designs, and new beginnings. Perception! Just as the mountain feels the pain of loss from the rains, lightning, snow, rock/mudslides, and fires, it also knows that it'll bring forth newness with a different beauty. We, too, need the same ability. We go through death, divorce, illness, loss of home or income, and many more tragedies. We all carry human scars. If we're to survive the devastations, then we, too, have to choose to see what the newness will bring. We don't get to stop things from happening to us, but we do get to choose how we want to perceive ourselves, others, and events. You are stronger than any event in your life. You have been given the ability to choose. Your perceptions, your beliefs, will create your facts. So, as they say, "Choose wisely."

When I see a mountain that has scars, I honor its strength and uniqueness. I see beauty in its unique rock formations, deep ravines, or places where whole parts of its origin are missing. It is through its flexibility that I see greatness. Through its constantly changing features, I see majesty and uniqueness.

Even though we are human beings, we have also witnessed some of the most incredible people of our time through understanding of their adversities and willingness to challenge, flex, and change. Look at the lives of Helen Keller, Nelson Mandela, Martin Luther King, and Mother Theresa, just to name a few. When we look to others who have overcome their adversities, we see the human potential to overcome our own. We have a responsibility to ourselves to be the best human beings we can be. We are the mountains that others look up to. People of the mountains know that whatever new challenge the mountain brings, it is only about perception, understanding, and time. Now, as I see the burned-out tree stumps covered in swaying grasses and a rainbow of wildflowers, I realize that it is just as beautiful as the forest once was.

Be flexible with life's uncertainties. Accept that change will happen—without your permission. Believe that you can create something even better—regardless of what's been handed to you.

Look Up To The Mountain. Challenge Your Flexibility.

INSIGHTS TO PONDER

1. What situations have you encountered that taught you about flexibility?
   - Write down a couple major situations. Ponder them for a moment.
   - Why did you choose to flex through it?
   - Looking at all the options, how did the option you chose outweigh the others? What were its benefits?

2. Have you ever felt victimized? (By the way, everyone has at one time or another.)
   - How did it feel?
   - While you were the victim, what were your thoughts?
   - What were your expectations for others to help you?
   - If you stayed in victimization for very long, what did you notice about your relationships?
   - To be the victim—was it beneficial or detrimental to you?
   - What kept you in it, or what got you out of it?

3. How did you learn to accept that you needed to be flexible to have a good life?
   - How has being flexible been helpful/hurtful to you?
   - What new things have you learned about you?
   - How have you applied what you've learned?

4. How have you become a better person?
    - List ten to fifteen positive personality traits that make up a *good person*.
    - Rate yourself from one (low) to ten (high) on each trait you've listed.
    - Is there a trait you could be working on? Could you add more traits to your list to hold yourself to?
    - What do you think people look up to you for?

NOTES

THE EAGLE

Ahh—to be an eagle
      soaring to great heights.
      never having to explain
      the reason for my flights.

Swooping and soaring,
freedoms to know,
searching and seeking
with winds that blow

Higher and higher,
there's no need to stop,
over mountains and rivers
till I've reached the top

Ahh—to be an eagle
      knowing freedoms so rare,
      believing in living
      with all fears to dare.

CHAPTER 4

COURAGEOUSLY BRAVE

MOUNTAINS MAKE US COURAGEOUS AND BRAVE

Extreme mountain climbers often speak to the difficulty of their climbs as being both physically and mentally exhausting. At times, each step reminds them of the fine line between life and death. Keeping focused and mentally overcoming both fear and physical pain is the only way they'll achieve the climb to the top. The mountain is the challenge, placed in your path to see if you have the stamina to continue. Without it, we'll never know what we're capable of doing, knowing, or being. It's the reason we're all here today. The fact that you're reading this says . . . you're alive! You've overcome whatever was necessary to be here today! I know that there have been difficult times when you've wondered if you'd make it through. Sometimes you've probably even wondered if you had the desire to do so. But something inside you wasn't ready to give up. You plodded along your way, one step at a time, until you arrived in a better place. You courageously conquered the mountain—but how? How were you able to do that?

Your thoughts are the most powerful creator of all. Your thoughts create an emotion, your emotion creates a physical/biological reaction, and then you have an action—you do or say something. All of that happens before you even react to the stimuli. If your thoughts are telling you that you'll get through this one step at a time, then they will create whatever you need to accomplish it. Your brain can do nothing more than what it's told to do. It's like a computer. What you program in is what you get out. The more you tell yourself something, the more your brain will create it into existence. Think of the ramifications of that statement. If you're a victim, your brain needs to make you see scenarios where you are continually victimized. It'll attract to you people who can victimize you, events where you can fail, and decisions you make only through the eyes of a victim, thus limiting your options. Or if you're telling yourself how content you are, your brain is busy helping you feel and see why you should be content—perhaps through gratitude or appreciation. That's the simple part.

Sometimes, though, we feel hijacked by our brain. Why am I reacting this way? I know better! I don't want to do this! Then you do it! What is that all about? Those are the messages you took in as a little person. It's a belief that says you're not safe, or adults are bad people, people you love hurt you, and so on. They run like an underground river, popping up when you least expect it. That's your subconscious. That's why therapists say you can change anything if you can bring it up to your conscious state. Once in your conscious mind, your thoughts can be redirected to benefit you, rather than create unsolicited grief. Here we're talking about the everyday human being who struggles, but has the cognitive ability to look at themselves, if or when necessary.

Your thoughts are so powerful that if you say, "I can't do this," your brain will start finding ways to make you give up, quit, or die. It's really that simple. If you want a quality life, you need to master your brain. It needs direction. It needs beliefs to hold onto. Brain autopilot is negative in nature. If you say, "I can't help it—that's just the way I am," then you are giving your brain permission to stay stuck. The hard part is that we don't want to always be responsible for our thoughts and actions. We want to take the easy way out and blame others or be the victim. It's easier. But the courageous will find a way to tell themselves that they won't accept defeat. They know that the difficulty will one day pass. So they put faith in their abilities knowing that they'll get through it. They repeatedly tell themselves that they *will* get through. Their thoughts are about "I can" versus "I can't" or "I won't." The brain helps to create the rest. *My* thoughts will create *my* belief, which will create *my* facts—period. It really is that simple, but it's difficult to master.

Have you ever told yourself over and over again how you want things different, but nothing seems to change? That's because we need to believe what we're telling ourselves. If we say one thing but believe something different, our brain says, "Which one is it?" It's getting two different messages. The brain will always default to the belief over your words. Try truly feeling what you're saying as truth. Give your brain specific examples. For example: I need to give a presentation. I'm really nervous. I keep telling myself I can do this with confidence and poise. But I don't feel confident. What's happening here? Most likely your brain is holding on to a painful memory. It may have been a very innocent memory—like standing up in front of a class, getting the answer wrong, and feeling humiliated as they laughed. If that's the case, I strongly suggest going to a therapist and try the Eye Movement Desensitization and Reprocessing (EMDR) technique. EMDR helps to clear up the emotion to that past memory and others associated with it. If you don't have time to get into a therapist, then try this: think of *any time* (not specific to your current situation) when you were successful (any kind of success). Feel the joy you felt in its accomplishment. Do several of these. Now you've specifically told your brain what you want by showing it past examples. You have now indicated to your brain what you expect as an outcome.

Another way to take away anxiety is to see how you would handle it if the worst did happen. What would you do? How would you react? How would you would handle it? Maybe, at first, you'd see yourself running out of the room, mortified. Do it again! How would you *want* to respond? See yourself pausing, maybe saying, "Excuse me," and then starting up again. Or maybe visualize laughing at yourself and saying, "Wow, there's a human moment," and then continue on. Try scenario after scenario until one feels right for you. Now you have problem-solved your worst fear and have acquired a solution. Practice it over and over again. The more you can trust your abilities, the less anxiety or depression you'll have. Again, believe in your abilities to handle any situation, see yourself as successful, believe that it's possible, and let your brain create the confidence you need.

Your thoughts are you! If I don't like what I'm thinking—if my thoughts are not helping me to the good—then I need to change them. There is no one on this planet who can make you change your thoughts if you're not open to it. You are the gatekeeper. Only with your permission can you change yourself, your life.

The first thing you need to do when you're climbing the mountain is *decide* whether or not you truly believe you can do it. Making that decision is the most powerful thing you can do. Decide! Set your thoughts on the path to accomplishment. The expert climbers don't start a climb until they know where their heads are at. Every mountain comes with difficulty somewhere along the way—rough terrain, weather, wildlife, whatever. Prepare your mind—how will you handle it *if*. . . ? This is exactly how our lives get played out. It doesn't matter what you need to tackle; decide first whether or not you're going to be successful. Then think about how to prepare for the difficulties you might run into. Figure out how you could handle the situations thrown at you. Then bravely move up your mountain.

Muster up your courage. Be brave enough to carry it out. Bravery is the action of courage. Bravery will help you accomplish what you want to do. Courage is knowing that there are fears and mentally tackling them. Bravery is creating the stamina to carry it out physically. Some people will stop at the first sign of trouble, but a brave person pushes on. Bravery doesn't let fear slow it down or stop it—it masters the fear. It doesn't mean that a person is not afraid; it means he or she will take on the challenge.

Once again, when your mind knows what it wants, it can overcome the obstacles. Have faith in your mind, your power, and your abilities, and you'll conquer any mountain that lies before you.

Be The Mountain—Be Courageous—Be Brave

INSIGHTS TO PONDER

1. Just like the professional climbers, we face obstacles. Sometimes the obstacles stop us from doing something that would be good for us. Can you remember a time when you knew what you needed to do but seemed stopped in your tracks when you tried to accomplish it?
   - Did you truly believe that you could accomplish it?
   - What made you brave enough to take that first step toward challenging yourself?
   - If you stopped yourself—didn't go through with it—how did that make you feel?
   - If you did carry it out, were you proud of yourself? How did that make you feel?

2. How do you handle fear?
   - List the things that you fear—physically, emotionally, and mentally.
   - Have you already challenged some of those fears? Which ones?
   - Looking at these fears, what would your next step be in mastery of each one of them?
   - Can you see how much you've already grown through the fears?
   - How has it been a benefit to you by taking these steps to master your fears?

3. Be aware of your thoughts and how they're guiding your life.
    - What negative things are you telling yourself about you?
    - What are you telling others about you—strengths and weaknesses?
    - Look into the future. You have mastered your greatest fears. What are you doing?
    - What are you telling or showing others now?
    - What are you telling yourself about your abilities?

4. What do you need to do to be a braver person in your own life?

NOTES

LIVING IN CONTRAST

You can't hold me down
because I desire to be—
Not by the standard of the whole
but by the freedom of the few.

With the sun upon my back,
    the snow at my feet,
With mountain after mountain,
    the plains succumb.
It's the valleys
    that make the mountains so tall.
It's the clouds
    that make the sky so blue.

No one can hold me down
because I want to be,
Nature has taught me.
Yet I live in a box—wanting to be free.

Photo Location: Slumgullion Pass, Lake City, Colorado

CHAPTER 5

BALANCE CREATED IN CONTRAST & OPPOSITES

THE MOUNTAINS CREATE BALANCE THROUGH UNDERSTANDING CONTRAST AND OPPOSITES

It's amazing to see the beautiful balance of a valley to a mountain. You can't help but wonder what great plan was in place—it's so huge, so incredible, so awe-inspiring. We're people who love balance. We talk about it all the time, we're searching for it all the time, and we think we're out of sync if we're not in it all the time. We look at shape, geometry, and color. The photographer loves the rule of thirds; a decorator looks at what makes a room pop; and the landscaper looks for flowing design. We see it in everything! We're looking at the color of a doctor's office, shape of a dress, the picture/word balance of an advertisement. We also look at balance for quality of life for ourselves. We look at what areas in our lives are getting either too much of our energy, or none at all. We'll see how we can make life more manageable by putting less energy into this and adding some into that. Yet when it's too calm and content, we get bored. The colors black and white make each other stand out because they're opposites, but add a little red, and, *wow*, now you have stimulation. Adding that splash of color is the contrast. The contrast is where we find excitement, passion, and stimulation. It's making our everyday get ramped up. We all live in a world based in opposites and contrasts.

So let's talk opposites. You can't have one side without the other side being present. For example: good versus bad, black versus white, left brain versus right brain, dependent versus independent, happy versus sad, or up versus down. Each side is important and powerful within its own right. They need each other. The valley needs the mountain to protect its grasses, the mountain needs the valley in order to look majestic and stable. As humans, our personalities and personal characteristics will also share the opposite sides. If you're very independent, then at some point in your life, you'll experience dependency. If you're kind, you have or will experience being mean. If you've had a great relationship, you've probably also had a difficult one. If you've felt on top of the world, you've probably also felt down in the dumps. It all goes hand in hand. We need to understand that each side teaches us something about ourselves. We need to experience both sides to have a perspective and determine for ourselves which side feels most like what we want. We always have choice! I often think about how much more I've learned from the downside than the upside. We are so busy trying *not* to experience the difficult side that we end up creating more of it.

Think of indulging parents. They're being overprotective and enabling because they genuinely want good things to happen for their child. Unfortunately, more often than not, it actually creates a young adult who can't solve problems or handle life. If the parents would let their child experience difficulties, he or she would grow up with coping skills, ideas on how to get through difficult times, and, most importantly, true self-esteem. By the way, true self-esteem is *only* gained by each individual working through his or her own ups and downs. True self-esteem comes from gaining the confidence and belief that you can handle whatever is thrown at you. If the American society would accept that difficulty is supposed to take place, we'd all be better for it. It's hard to change when our society believes that everyone should *always* be happy, healthy, and safe. That's the constant that we strive for. We should be striving for experiences of all kinds, to stretch our abilities and beliefs. We need to spend less time in avoiding and whining and more time in embracing and contemplating for insights. No one out there can define you unless you choose not to do your own work. Then, and only then, have you given up your power for someone else to control.

Look around you. Notice old sayings—for example, "Opposites attract." They do—that person is your own personal teacher, and you are his or hers. It would be way too boring otherwise. Look at these pairings; mean people find kind people, controlling people find those who are victims, and people with low self-esteem usually find the narcissists. Remember, every person is on a continuum. We all can be kind—we all can be mean. It's often based on how often and how intense we want to make it.

Those who consciously choose to be more in the middle become the most powerful humans there are. They are not deterred by difficulty, and neither are they overly expectant of joy and happiness. These people understand that all experiences are beneficial. The positive side is not any greater than the downside—it is just different. Let's say I decide to be a compassionate person; then every (hard or easy) scenario will present itself with the opportunity to be compassionate. I may get to practice using my compassion for a baby animal or toward a yelling, angry person who needs to be understood. If I've decided that I'm a victim, then every scenario will present opportunities to be just that. I will marry a person who shuts me down so I can feel helpless and powerless. Or, I'll get a job with a boss who puts me down in front of my staff. Or, I'll only see the discourteous drivers on the highway and feel the frustration that there's nothing I can do. Remember that the brain can only do what you've told it to do. If I've decided I'm compassionate—my brain will show me opportunities of practice. Practice means within the opposite sides. This, of course, is very simplistic, knowing we have thousands of characteristics and beliefs.

But hopefully you get the picture of how we need to work with our brain, not against it, to help ourselves. You'll see opposites happening everywhere. Seriously, just pay attention. You'll see the rich losing money, the intelligent getting dementia, the healthy becoming sick. It's not a bad thing; it's the way our world works—so get busy working through things instead of fighting it and believing it shouldn't happen to you. If you have a difficulty, look and see if you've experienced it on the good side. If not, it'll be coming your way at some point. It helps to be grateful for the spectrum. It can give you hope, knowing you'll get through. You can say, when you're on the difficult side, that it was fun on the upside, so now you know that this difficulty is only completing the cycle. Watch through a different lens—one of acceptance and capability rather than victimization and powerlessness.

Thus, in keeping balance, you don't need to go to one side or the other, because the more you're at one end, the more you're creating the opposite end. If you're a person who loves severe highs and lows, then that's okay, too. Most people really don't. Content, joyful, and grateful can feel just as powerful as excited, thrilled, and exhilarating. In life, there really isn't a true balanced state that's permanent. You can find it in the *now* while doing meditation, yoga, and so on. But for everyday life, just look for what brings you more joy and contentment. When difficulties come, get through them as fast as you can and move on.

Remember that in art, a simple color or a line can make a huge change. Contrast to anything can create an eye-popping experience. In our human lives, we may need to create something new, especially to stay out of boredom. So add a passion. Explore a new book or a new concept. Try something different you've never done before. Collect some quotes that are meaningful to you, and then contemplate how that applies in your everyday life. Challenge yourself, and you'll add the eye-popping color needed to give your life a positive boost.

Last but not least, understand that you will experience both sides of the coin at some point. That's truly how this planet runs. Neither side can exist without the other. You can't make great decisions for yourself if you don't understand both sides. Each side is a teacher for you to become the best *you* that you can become.

Be The Mountain Of Balance, Through Understanding The Gift Of Opposites And Contrast

INSIGHTS TO PONDER

1. Looking back at your life, can you see where you have experienced both sides of the world of opposites? Look at it through your relationships, jobs, health, passions . . . Write down what opposites you see. How about your personality characteristics?

2. Looking at your life, where do you see the most balance? What makes it stay in balance or fall out of balance? What does balance really mean to you? If you see areas in your life that really could use some balancing, how will you do that?

3. What are your expectations for happiness? What happens if you don't meet your expectations? If you need to handle your expectations of happiness differently, what would you do?

4. Are you doing a lot of the same old things, day in and day out? How could you spice them up? What kind of contrasts could you throw in there to make life a bit more interesting?

5. Do you believe that others make your life good or difficult? How does your responsibility to "making a better you" through balance, contrast (stimulation), and understanding of opposites create your life today? How about your future?

MY MASKS

For I, the I you do not see
Is the I that feels—the real me.

I've used my knowledge to hide my fears
And used my laughter to hide my tears.

You think you know who I might be?
Did you ever think that there's more to me?

How happy I must appear to be
To all those wanting not to see.

But look now and you'll be aware
Of the many masks that I can wear.

CHAPTER 6

UNIQUE YET STABLE

MOUNTAINS TEACH US ABOUT BEING UNIQUE

When I look at the whole range of mountains, I'm in awe of their unique features. Each mountain seems to tell its own story—different from all the rest. Each of their cores is very similar, yet each is unique in many other ways. It is solid at its base with many of the same minerals. Its basic structure will be around for millions of years yet to come. We know—we can believe and have faith in its future existence. It's a comforting thought. We humans love our stability and security but are hell-bent on our uniqueness.

We're not much different from the mountains. We were all born with a grounding factor—our personality. We can smooth it or enhance it, but the main personality is still there. We have a sense about who we are. That's the core person others seldom get to see, but you know it exists. We work at making the rough parts better, the scarred parts bearable, and the great parts even greater. What makes us unique, just like the mountain, is what happens on the surface. Just like what happens to the mountains, each sadness, tragedy, or pain creates a ravine. Some ravines are so deep and treacherous that no one can go into them. Each time an emotional theme hits again and again, the ravine gets deeper and deeper. Over time bushes and rocks fill it up, but the ravine is still there. Its depth is way too painful to allow exploration. It simply exists until time changes it—or someone is willing to carefully challenge it. Sometimes the hurts are so traumatic that a part of us falls away, just like a mudslide, still there but displaced. It leaves a scar so large we can't move forward—frozen in time—it has defined us. It has become our current living history.

Moving forward can be more about survival and caution than carefree joys and freedom. In the caution zone, it is difficult to trust and share your true feelings or opinions and ideas. In survival mode, you learn to play life safe. The needs will be met by only you, as it's not safe to let anyone else in. It's asking you to be in control of yourself—always. The fear supersedes the needs. No matter how much you want that relationship or that job or that new friend, your subconscious will protect you based on *your* history. Out of fear, it'll sabotage your wants, it'll create chaos in your desires, or it'll overwhelm you until you need to shut down all your hopes and dreams. Just like the rains, lightning, snows, and fires changed the mountains, so, too, does our self-image and how others see us change with scarring. It's the historical scars on our bodies, in our hearts, and in our minds that are our watchdogs, never allowing us a chance to be hurt again. Our subconscious is made to protect us from hurting. It will not allow a potential or future possibility in. Therefore, it will only meet your needs and keep you stuck. Challenging your fears (what you are telling yourself), will allow new possibilities and potential thoughts to arrive. You will be able to see things differently, and hopefully open the doors. The core in *you* knows you want to be free of the historical scars and become open to new possibilities.

The core of the mountain stands strong. The core knows that no matter what happens on the outside, the inside is still as strong as ever. We, as humans, are also strong in our core. It believes in our potential to overcome. The difference is how we choose to see it. Are we helpless to environmental changes? Can we roll with the punches? Can we see ourselves as unique instead of damaged? Can we look back and see what we've learned about ourselves, others, beliefs we've held, or knowledge gained?

When I see all the scarring, I see beauty, uniqueness, survival, and strength. The more scarring, the more unique—the more it should be honored. It is deserving of my awe, not my pity. The mountain is a warrior standing strong for everyone else to see. It acknowledges its pain and makes itself beautiful anyway.

Everyone on this planet is going to get scarred. So maybe your strength comes from standing with a group with like scars, like a mountain range, or maybe standing alone, quietly rising above the plains. No matter how you find your strength, all paths are worthy of self-love, honor, and awe—awe in the beauty of whom you became in spite of what was thrown at you.

We need to develop a sense of respect for each person's journey, not to judge it or fill it with expectations, but to just honor it. Your scars are your badge of courage. Your environment has helped to create the incredible, unique you. It doesn't matter how it happened; it matters how tall you stand through it. You have been very busy creating a beautiful, unique person. The most inspiring majestic mountains are the most unique and rugged. Yes, they have their scars, but they are exceptional. They have weathered their lives majestically. You, too, can choose to see yourself in the same way. See yourself as majestic and exceptional, regardless of what has happened to you through life. *You* are worthy of awe!

Be The Mountain—Unique And Exceptional.

INSIGHTS TO PONDER

1. Write down what makes you unique.

2. Look at that list. How do you view yourself *now*, as you ponder each of those situations that made you unique?
   - What did you learn about life from that experience?
   - What was the hardest part to get through, and why?
   - What skills and/or abilities did you use to help you through it? Do you still use those coping strategies today?
   - Looking back do you wish you would have done something differently? If so, what, and why?

3. Looking at the photographs in this book: which mountain do you relate to the most?
   - What is it about the mountain that you relate to? If the mountain had emotions, how would it be feeling?
   - How do your own feelings relate to those of the mountain?

4. Looking into the future, how do you anticipate getting through difficulties? How would you hope to view yourself after it's over? How have you learned to *honor* your life and respect your journey?

UPON THE MOUNTAIN

Upon the mountain
> a view to behold,
> the breeze blowing by.

I feel love,
> a joy of respect,
> no questioning why.

A human being
> desires to be loved
> yet only cries.

I feel confused,
> withdrawn understanding;
> questions seemingly pry.

Why is it
> I can love a mountain
> and know that it is real?

Why is it
> I can see a friend
> and know not how I feel?

CHAPTER 7

RESPECT ALL THINGS

THE MOUNTAIN DESERVES RESPECT

The first thing I think about when I see a mountain is respect. That mountain was here long before I came around, and it will continue to be there long after I die. It has weathered time, erosion, and destruction. It's easy to respect its scars. But the mountain deserves respect because it exists. Everything in nature deserves equal respect to human beings. We think we're at the top of all living and nonliving things. We make all the decisions about how life will be on this planet. But really, it makes us the most vulnerable. Being the human being doesn't mean that we get to sit in the comfy cozy chair being waited on. No—it means we have the greatest responsibility to keep all the living things below us healthy and happy so *we* can be healthy and happy. The higher we are, the more dependent we are on those below us. We have an obligation to listen to our world and help out in its distress.

BE THE MOUNTAIN

Living in Colorado, we see how the beetles have killed our beautiful pine trees. It's overwhelming to see thousands of acres turn orange and die. It's emotional! It makes us want to help in some way. But we need to be careful how we decide to react. Do we find a new chemical to destroy the beetles (and maybe other things in the process), or do we let Mother Nature take care of herself? We have a hard time just letting it go—we love to be in control. We love our trees—what if they all die? Mother Nature may have a different plan. She may be making new space to enhance the soil for new growth to keep herself healthy in the future. It doesn't mean that we're supposed to intervene—we're obligated to see all sides. If the solution is too difficult, then maybe it's not supposed to be the path. Here's a human scenario: if a company is trying to come up with a new product and has setback after setback, it's probably the wrong direction. Perhaps they have trouble hiring staff, and then difficulty getting the right facility, and then trouble getting the right equipment. One problem after another says, "Not the right time, the right people, or the right issue." *At that time,* the decision is moving in the wrong direction; sit back get more information. There may be something you missed in your haste.

Nature knows a whole lot more than we give her credit for. Respect is earned. Who do you think creates the tsunamis, earthquakes, rockslides, thunderstorms, beetles killing the pines? We, as humans, generally just see the momentary need. But nature sees a need for change for her healthy survival. We need to listen more, sit back for a moment or two, and challenge ourselves to think about the worst/best scenarios. Let's try to see the big picture, even if it's uncomfortable. Nobody wants to lose the trees, but new growth will occur for many, many, years down the road. New, healthier forests will rise. Then the cycle will repeat itself again. It is a simple yet complex process where Mother Nature always wins.

She's really the one in control. Just about the time we're feeling pretty good about our sense of control over her, she comes in and challenges the rules we've just made. She puts us back in our place. The mountains are a perfect example of her control. She built them out of upheaval. We now are blessed with ranges of mountains and all that they provide. She knew that in the long run, it would bring much joy to our planet, even though the upheaval was painful. She reminds us that there are always many factors, besides ourselves, that make a world healthy.

Nature can take care of herself with the things that she creates. She can't take care of the things that we create. So if what we've created hurts the earth, then it is our duty to stop it—rethink what we're doing and correct it. If we leave her out of healthy decision making, then we will have to take the consequences, however those may look. We get back what we've created—let's be careful of what it is that we create. Be respectful and create goodness for the earth so she can thrive and be healthy for all of us.

Be The Mountain Based In Respect Of All Things

INSIGHTS TO PONDER

1. What kinds of things do you need to control? Is it helpful or hurtful to someone or something else?

2. Can you remember a time when you did something in the moment, perhaps not thinking it through, and it benefitted you, but in the long run, it hurt someone or something else?
   - How did that feel?
   - Looking back, if you had made a different decision, how would things look now?

3. If you were in charge of this planet, what would you change to better the chances in the future for all living and nonliving things?

4. Is it okay to have extinction?
   - Would it be okay for something to become extinct while in our care?
   - Where would humans be if no extinctions had occurred on this planet?

5. Mother Earth has been around forever.
   - How do you respect what she has given to you thus far?
   - How do you show your respect?
   - What area in your life do you need to respect more, just because it exists?

6. How do you know if you've had one too many roadblocks?
   - Do you quickly change your mind?
   - At what point do you stop and get more information?

7. Here's a thought: if you're concerned about something, and you're asking a lot of questions about it, then you stop and get more information. Don't make that decision! When you've answered the issue well enough you'll feel solid in your answer. The fewer the questions left, the more solid the decision. I used to tell clients, "If you go to the refrigerator and ask "What am I hungry for?" close the door – because you're not hungry. When you're hungry, you open the door, you'll know exactly what you want!" Asking the question means it's time to research and educate—you need more information.

NOTES

MY WORLD?

What are these things
I have to face—
this world of mine
seems out of place.

This life I play
        the world I see
The games that stay—
        is it you or me?
The words I say—
        are they real or fake?
Thought for the day—
        how much did we make?

What are these things
that set our pace,
where love must fight
to keep its base?

Photo Location: Lake Königssee, Salzburg, Austria

CHAPTER 8

SUCCESS

THE MOUNTAINS HELP US DEFINE SUCCESS

It's the high, unforgiving mountains that give us society's description of success. Success symbolizes the top—the few. Mountain climbers will tell you how difficult it is to get to the top, its challenge increasing with each step. Many people will start the trek, but few will complete it. Why is that? If success is for only those who get to the top, then the rest of us are doomed before we start! I just can't buy that! Success to me is if I can say I've had a lot more great than difficult, or more smiles than tears, more challenges than roadblocks. That is success!

We know that everyone has a different level of perseverance, pleasure markers, and abilities. Everyone has a different reason for starting the *successful* climb. Some may do it because friends asked them to, some will do it to see if they can complete it, and some, out of curiosity, may want to see what the view is from the top. Some may start on the path knowing that the intent isn't to reach the top but rather to enjoy the journey for as far as it may take them.

Success is very much the same way. We can all see the mountaintop. Society shows us, every day, those who have made it, who are successful. We can see the path that leads to the top. We've been shown the stairsteps to get where others have gone. No matter what we've been shown, each of us will take the journey for a different reason. For example, in a work situation some may do it for better pay; some will do it for a competitive challenge; some may do it because they like the boss; and some may do it to see what they're capable of achieving.

For some reason, we're all taught that we should all want to be on top of the mountain. Yet we know that most people don't want success for the same reason; it's a unique person setting a unique goal. We judge ourselves and others according to our own perception of what makes a person successful. When we don't trust our own perceptions, we compare ourselves to others who are closer to the top; then we wonder why we're not making it. Then we get back on the path and keep plodding along, all the while knowing this just isn't us. Why do we do that to ourselves? My dreams and goals may have nothing to do with your dreams and goals. My intentions are not your intentions. If a nurse wants to work directly with patients but then gets promoted to administration, he/she has now changed the purpose of why he or she goes to work each day. If this person can't find a new purpose within what he or she is now asked to do, there can only be conflict. The conflict will appear both inwardly and outwardly. Eventually this person will become so unhappy with everything around him or her that change will have to occur. We're so busy getting caught up in what everyone else thinks our success path should look like that we forget to ask ourselves, "What was my reason for wanting to do this in the first place? Does it still align with the original purpose? Am I ready for a new purpose? What is the essence of this internal conflict? Will it challenge my true purpose or take it down a path that feels misdirected?" Only you can answer these questions—do not ask others for their advice. They do not know what your original intent was; they do not know what success means to you or how you judge your successfulness! Be strong enough to ask yourself questions, and then listen to your gut *before* your head convinces you differently (a conscious/rational takeover). We are given both intuition and knowledge. We need to use both. Use your intuition first, and then see if the facts validate it. If not, perhaps you need more information, either in intuition (which means paying attention to your feelings) or knowledge (do some research).

If I've climbed some distance up the mountain and have seen the beauty along the way, do I need to go to the top? If I sit at the bottom of the mountain, watching the creek flow by, is my experience any less than that of someone who made it to the top? *My* mountain, *my* way! Success is only relevant to you and the reason you chose to be there.

Make every trek—every experience—a meaningful one. If it is meaningful, you will always feel its fullness and completeness, no matter where you are on the path. And by the way, at the top of the mountain, there are strong winds, no shade, lightning, and unending loose rocks! Get the picture? Know what you are climbing for. Be in alignment with yourself; know your intentions. Stop when the pleasure no longer exists; sit and be quiet; ask questions to your soul. If necessary, find a new path or make a new intention/purpose—the rest will fall into place.

Honor your intentions, intuition, and knowledge based on *your* definition of success!

Be On Your Mountain Of Success

INSIGHTS TO PONDER

1. Think about success:
   - How do you personally define success?
   - From 0 percent (low) to 100 percent (high): how would you rate your success in life so far?
   - Why did you choose that rating?
   - Where do you struggle with success in your life?
   - What successes stand out in your life?
   - Looking into the future, what will you look back and say you were successful at?

2. Have you ever started up a path of success and decided it wasn't really what you wanted and therefore stopped the climb?
   - How did you feel?
   - Were others trying to convince you to stay the course?
   - Write down anything you'd like to say about how you've become successful today.

3. How do you show that you're the living proof of success? How do you walk your talk?

4. If you're not as successful as you thought you'd be, why not?

5. Is your purpose for being where you are in life being fulfilled?

6. If not, what's a step to take that can start fulfillment?

7. Looking back at your rating, what rating would you like to say you achieved before you die?

NOTES

IF I'M OPEN

Nature has given the best to me,
holding high her philosophies.
Oh, open my mind,
    and let me see!
I sit here quietly, aware:
    the woodpecker
    the ants
    the winds
    the moisture filled air . . .
I can feel them,
    hear them,
    sense them . . .
I sit here, silently aware . . .
    swollen rivers,
    musty mine shafts,
    moss-covered rocks,
    new spring leaves,
    How will they fare?

Yes, nature has given the best to me,
    Connected and loving,
    If I choose to see.

CHAPTER 9

BE QUIET—BE STILL

THE MOUNTAINS REMIND US TO BE QUIET—BE STILL

If you sit and observe the mountains, you'll notice a stillness, a quietness, around them. They are massive giants, yet quiet and alone. At their base, notice how they are deeply connected to the earth and to one another. The widest part of the mountain is where it is grounded. There, it is strong and steadfast. Notice how, as you look higher, up to its peak, it becomes narrower and independent of the other mountains around it, each peak having its own unique character. We, too, are strong and steadfast in our grounding, yet free and independent of one another. It is in our grounding that we can acquire our freedom. If we lose our grounding, we lose our true freedom.

The mountains look as if they are the silent guards of nature. They are the patrons of protection. They watch over the valleys and canyons. Their bases are strong together, unflappable. We, too, need to protect those ideals that make us unique: our beliefs, our character, our tragedies, and our history. We get to choose who receives our information. Hence, the freedom, like the tops of the mountains. We must protect our inner being from being trampled on, told we are wrong to think or believe as we do, or save ourselves from humiliation. We have the freedom to decide *who* gets the information, *when* they get the information, or *if* the information should be shared at all. Listen to yourself first and then make a decision based on who, what, or how to hare that information.

Be the sentry of your life! Notice yourself with others. How do you handle the difficulties, or who are you around when you're at your best or worst? If you don't quiet yourself, you won't learn to listen. You won't hear the greatest intelligence you've been given: intuition and internal self-guidance. Be watchful and observe yourself. Be still; get above your troubles and just see where it might take you. Maybe you'll decide to do a do-over, see a new option, or just take a single step in a different direction. It's your freedom to create, once you've listened.

Pay attention as you watch over you. Could anyone really watch over you better than you? Is it really anyone else's responsibility to be watchful over you? It's your responsibility to be the most independent person you can be while staying attached to humankind. If you are in a relationship to be taken care of, *you* need to rethink your responsibility to yourself and/or your partner. We need to figure out our own needs and how to take care of them. If you're in a needs-based relationship, what will you do if you or your partner's needs change? The only way that relationship will work is if both people are flexible enough to flow into the next set of needs. If one chooses not to, then the relationship ends. Know your own needs; be still and listen.

In your stillness you can hear your soul/intuition instead of your head. Your intuition knows your mission here and will gently guide you—if you let it. In our fast-paced lifestyles, we've learned to be afraid of silence. You can always text, tweet, or look on Facebook just to keep yourself from having to sit with yourself—alone. So put the technology away—find a quiet place. Contemplate your life. Who are you, and where are you going? If you died tomorrow, what would people say about you? What do you believe makes a good person? How are you living up to that?

If you don't learn to protect yourself, your time, and your energy, you, like the mountain, will crumble away and deteriorate like the piles of rock at the bottom. Sometimes, it's important to be the rock pile at the bottom so it can jolt us to wake up and be mindful of oneself. This reminds me of driving on the mountain roads. Sometimes you'll see just a few rocks that have broken away from the hillside laying in the middle of the road. You can easily get around them and continue on your journey. But other times there's a rockslide, and you need to wait for help or go a totally different direction. Just like the mountains, at first we may just feel a little low, a little drained, or a little lethargic. We kind of go around it and tell ourselves just keep on going in our chaotic lives. However, if you keep this up for long, guess who gets the rockslide? Your body will shut you down—all because you aren't paying attention to your core, your grounding. You're not paying attention to you—to your true responsibility. Learn to be quiet, be still, and listen. Protect your soul so that you may soar, standing free and independent.

Be The Mountain—Quiet And Still

INSIGHTS TO PONDER

1. Like the mountain, how do you ground yourself?

2. Why is it important to you to be grounded? In other words, how do you maintain solidness or security within your being, day by day?

3. How do you protect yourself—your beliefs, ideas, options, deep feelings? Who do you share or not share information and why? Do you honor your decision or try to override it (and get burned, again)?

4. How do you quiet your thoughts?

5. How do you quiet your emotions?

6. Have you changed your process over the years? What works now?

7. How do you take care of you?

A DREAMED REALITY

As I sat by the river
        one warm, sunny day,
I felt it wash my mind away
        to a place I'd never been before.

        A dreamed Reality?
        Could this be Reality?

I felt the wind
        blow through my hair.
It searched my mind to find nowhere;
        my thoughts were someplace out of time.

        A dreamed Reality?
        This dream is my precious reality!

CHAPTER 10

DREAMS AND THE BIG PICTURE

THE MOUNTAINS SHOW US THE BIG PICTURE AND DREAMS

One thing I've noticed about having a view is that you need to be on a hill, a mountain, or something that's taller than the valley or plains. It doesn't have to be a 14,000-footer to get an awesome view. My family's cabin, on a Colorado mountain, was only at 8,600 feet, and it had a spectacular view of a mountain range, valleys, and rivers. When I was in Kansas, a small hill had a great view of fields upon fields of wheat and sunflowers. When I hiked the Grand Canyon, the rim offered an impressive view below me. So why is it important to see an overview of where we are?

There are times in our lives when we need to see the bigger picture—not only to find our way, but also to create dreams. When I stand on a mountaintop, I feel stronger, more alive, and my troubles seem smaller. At that moment, I'm a piece of a larger plan. I can't help but see my troubles in a different way—it's like magic. My problem-solving skills are opened and ready for new experiences, new thoughts, and new feelings. I notice that I'm more capable, more willing to learn something new or just sit, being open to contemplate my future. There's something about open space—vastness—that puts the mind and heart in the same place. We open our minds, think greater thoughts, delve into greater philosophies, and question it all. How can one sit on a cliff overlooking an ocean, or the mountain, or the Grand Canyon, and not sense the vastness of life?

Somehow it takes us away from our daily routines and methodical thoughts. In that space, we can dream, rethink a situation, or ask deeper questions of ourselves and our world. That starts the process of dreaming. When I ask questions about making myself a better person or doing more for my world, I've opened the door for opportunity. Creative ideas start popping into my head. The open space offers my logical mind new opportunities to challenge what I know.

The right side of our brain was made to express itself through sensitivities, creativity, and abstractions. It thrives in open space. It feels awe, feels a thought, or smells the flower blooming next to where you're sitting. The right brain learns through the five senses: sound, sight, smell, taste, and touch. So maximize your right brain potential by putting yourself in a scenario that enhances the senses. Let your brain work for you by putting yourself in an expansive place. Ideas will start to flow into you, because that's the gift of the right brain! The right brain is made to question everything. Who are you, really? Why do you follow certain rules/laws and not others? Why are we the only people on a planet? Why or why not save the trees? If you open the door, the questions will come. It's a wonderful place for curiosity.

The downside to a strong right brain is the side that must be mastered. The downside? Decision making. You are getting so many new thoughts, ideas, and feelings that you're afraid you'll miss out—something better might come along. It can paralyze you for fear of making a wrong decision, or binding you to a commitment you regret. It can self-sabotage quickly, sending you down the path of boredom and depression. Not a fun place to go—so we learn to master its downside and elevate its good side. It needs to find a way to express itself that is beneficial to self and others. If you have a dominate right brain, then you're a feeling, creative soul. Learn about your abilities and your downsides. Master what hurts you and develop what helps you. Most importantly, we *all* have a right brain—so we all need to pay attention to ways of enhancement.

To those of you who have a dominating left brain, you'll seek comfort through processes, details, and order. You like the box of habits and routines. Just like the right-brainers, you, too, have a downside that needs to be mastered as you have a tendency to make everything too logical. Even your sense of humor is sarcastic and complicated. Your gift is logic. Things have rhyme and reason—it has to make sense. Your mastery is your heart and feelings. It's being able to let go and find enjoyment out of things that are different, new options, or flexing with change. It's the mastery of hearing new possibilities without judging its correctness (usually based in your history, as you have an incredible memory!). Challenge yourself—do something different just because you can. To find out about left/right brain dominance, just go online and search left/right brain tests, or go to your local library or bookstore, as they'll have books on the concept.

So what does all this have to do with the bigger picture and dreaming? Well, there's a reason we have two sides of our brain. The dominate side seems natural—you don't have to work at it; it just flows easily. The other side is to be mastered, making it a benefit to you. We need to learn to use both sides with equal flexibility. We get the choice to stimulate it or starve it. Either way, you're creating *you*!

Put your right brain to work. Open your mind and see things in a different way. Stimulate your brain by asking deeper questions. Put yourself in a sensory extravaganza, enhancing your journey. Let the dreams arie from out of nowhere. Be open to the possiblities it brings. Stand at the top of your mountain and dream. With those dreams, decide on your first step to fulfilling them—then do it!

__Be The Mountain—Stimulating Openness, Depth, And Dreams__

INSIGHTS TO PONDER

1. When was the last time you sat in an elevated place?
   - What did it feel like?
   - What were your thoughts about?
   - When you left, what did you feel?
   - Is there something you could have done to maximize that experience?

2. Take a left/right brain test (go online and type in Left-Right brain tests). Sometimes, when taking these tests, it's easier to think back to when you were in grade school through high school. As we age we have mastered a great deal about out ourselves so that it's difficult to determine which is natural and which is mastered.

3. Contemplate something crazy. Right-brainers can create easily but get stuck in choosing one—left-brainers have to really work at the creation —but try it anyway. Pay attention to how you're feeling or what you're thinking while doing this.

4. Has *being open* to new options been beneficial to you? How?

5. Has *being open* ever created a disappointment or felt negative? If so:
   - What did you do?
   - How did you handle it?
   - How did it turn out?
   - How did you internalize it?
   - What impact has that made now? Future?

6. Where would you go to if you needed to feel more open, more creative?

COME WITH ME, MY FRIEND

Come with me, my friend,
Love what you can't see.
Feel the majestic mountains
Swelling golden flowers with pride.

Come with me, my friend,
Feel how you can love.
Find the broken bluebird's egg
Seeking compassion from human eyes.

Come with me, my friend,
Learn who you might be.
Seek contentment and wonder
In nature's love and passionate signs.

CHAPTER 11

BE UPLIFTING

MOUNTAINS ARE UPLIFTING

As we look to the mountains, we see that we must look up to them. We are so small in comparison. If we compare ourselves to the mountains, we'll always feel like we're "less than." Everyone, at some point in his or her life, has felt small. Maybe it was poor self-esteem, or you were ashamed of something you did or said, or you felt inadequate. The list can go on and on. Everyone, at some point in his or her life, needs to be uplifted. Life can be difficult through no fault of our own. It just is what it is.

We are all capable of helping someone else feel better. There is no magic wand. There is no right way to say something. This comes from the heart and doesn't require that it be done right or perfect. We need to empower, encourage, and lift up our family, friends, and strangers. Never underestimate a simple act or gesture. That simple act may be the one thing that saves someone's life.

BE THE MOUNTAIN

I'll never forget a story that was told to me from a client, in his forties, about the simple act of a smile. He remembered being a teenager having the worst time of his life. He decided that enough was enough. He had tried to hide it so that others wouldn't interfere with his newfound plan. His plan—to go home that night and hang himself. He just couldn't take life anymore. He believed that family and friends had let him down so often that he just couldn't count on anyone anymore. He was certain no one would miss him anyway. As he was leaving school, a student he didn't know just smiled at him. It was warm and caring. She made eye contact that felt deep and genuine. He knew he really didn't want to die—he was just tired of being sad and lonely. He just couldn't think of anything else to do. As he walked home, he began to cry. Maybe, just maybe, there was a possibility of hope. He realized how powerful that smile had been. He thought about it and then thought some more. He finally decided to give smiling a try, just to see if what he felt could be validated again, or if it had just been a quirk. He wasn't giving up his plan to die; it was just put on temporary hold. It was a dim hope but it was something. He felt like he could smile at strangers because they wouldn't know him. It wouldn't make a difference—no interaction was necessary. It was a simple step that he didn't put much credence in. Yet he started smiling at strangers, slowly at first, maybe just a few times a day. As he smiled, people smiled back. It actually felt good. He realized that getting smiles back helped him to feel a little bit better each day. He got to the point where he looked forward to smiling. He regained a sense of emotional control in his life. He got to choose whom he smiled at, when he decided to smile, and what kind of smile to use. Many times he chose to smile at the underdogs—just like the person he felt he was. He learned a vital step in self-survival—a coping strategy.

Smiling didn't take away all his pains, but it gave him a temporary way to find a sense of purpose. It became important to become a kind person. Sometimes we need to *be* what we want to receive. When he decided to smile at others, he took back his power that he had let others take away. That decision, based on a smile from a stranger, literally saved his life. He never got to know her, but he'll never forget her warm smile. He turned out to be an awesome human being. It would have been a great loss to this world had he carried out his plan. He has helped so many people since—it's hard to imagine he was ever in a suicidal position.

Maybe we don't need to have such a drastic lesson. Challenge yourself. You'll be amazed at how good it feels when most people acknowledge your smile by smiling back. I had this happen to me one day, about a month ago. A lady in the grocery store stopped me just to tell me how beautiful my smile was. I was on cloud nine the rest of the day. She validated me. She took an extra minute out of her day to say something nice to me. Here simple comment made me want to smile even more! We all need to spend more time by empowering people who are doing something positive, no matter how small it might seem.

When we learn how to rise above our own sadness, disappointments, and sorrows, we need to help others out of theirs. It's called "going full circle." We don't withhold caring, loving, or honoring. It is a wisdom to know about ourselves and then learn to share it with others in a way that's nonjudgmental or haughty. Don't be judgmental and critical "for their own good"; it's not for you to judge, as we seldom know where they're *really* coming from. I've seen some of the happiest people (on the outside) carrying the gravest of emotions on the inside. You would never know—they'd never let you see their pain. Don't assume that you know what's best for them; we all wear a lot of masks to cover pain, sadness, and discouragement—just give a warm smile.

Role-modeling or inspiring someone has great power as well. Inspiration is about lifting up one's spirit, one's soul. It's about giving hope and a new option to consider. Stand proud, like the mountain, and share your wisdom. Take a small action. *Do* something to make someone else's day. Not as a dictator telling others how they should be, but as a loving human being *allowing* them to be. Your job is to be the best you. Letting yourself shine gives others around you permission to do the same.

This is not only a challenge but a responsibility to humankind. We all belong to the same human race. We are all a piece of each other. We have all felt the pains of sorrow, discouragement, lost loves, and unfairness. We all know how bad it can feel. When we listen, we can then encourage or empower someone else to be stronger. Do you have a story? Share it with someone else going through something similar. Share how you got through it. In the long run, it's not just about that one person. The ripple effect is the energy that changes many people, even nations, and a world. You will never know the true impact your kindness, caring, honoring, and compassion will do. You do it because you can, not because it's easy or convenient. You can make a huge difference by just starting with a smile. Take the time to smile at a stranger, help someone in need, or just listen to someone's story.

Be The Mountain That Others Can Look Up To!
Then—Lift Up: Inspire, Encourage, Empower.

INSIGHTS TO PONDER

1. When was the last time you complimented a stranger? Smiled at a stranger?

2. Can you remember a time when someone (who didn't have to) really helped you out? How did it feel?

3. Have you ever helped someone out who really needed it (but you didn't have to)? How did that feel?

4. In our busy lives, we often forget to empower or encourage. Make a pact with yourself to do it more often. Maybe just compliment someone on a smile, or you just smile more.

5. Many times throughout our lives, we won't get our needs met through others. If you become what you want (and you're not getting it from others), soon you won't need others to do it for you. You'll already be fulfilled. *Practice* giving what you want. Not just once—do it many times. Others will see your change, and they'll start changing, too. Be the kind of person you want others to emulate. Above all, just smile more. *Practice!*

NOTES

SHINE SOFTLY, MY FRIENDS

Shine softly, my friends,
And you'll be amazed
How showing a caring gesture
Can set the world ablaze.

Shine softly, my friends,
And you will understand
How a simple act in love
Brings joy to all of man.

Shine softly, my friends,
Choosing loving ways to be
Will bring changes one by one.
Open your hearts—you'll see.

Choose to Shine—Softly

ACKNOWLEDGMENTS

Along my life's journey, many have been there to help support and encourage me. Some have played a short, impactful part, and others have been there for most of my life. Impactful is impactful, no matter how long the stay. I know I can't mention everyone, so my apologies upfront for those I haven't included. Please know that you are cherished in my life, and I will be forever grateful for the friendships and love that we share.

To Hunts, the love of my life, my husband and cherished life friend: From the day we met, thirty-seven years ago, we were brought together through our hearts. You have encouraged my independence, my curiosities, and my knowledge. You have never asked me to step back into a role or to be less than what I am. Your genuine love is shown daily. I trust you with every inch of my body and soul. There are no words to thank you for that feeling of trust and belief in someone. I am so appreciative that you allow the space for me . . . to just be me. Thank you for your love, support, humor, encouragement, and understanding. I love you with all my heart—truly beyond words.

To my sister Cindy: not only are you my biological sister, you are the greatest friend anyone could have. We truly are "soul twins." We can laugh till we cry or encourage and motivate each other to great achievements. Through supporting one another, we love and respect each other at the deepest soul level. You are my spiritual confidant, allowing me to explore without judgment or expectations. I am so grateful that we live close to each other and have the opportunity to spend a lot of time together doing wild and crazy things. I cherish our time. I am so proud to be called your sister. Love you on all levels forever.

To my brother Wayne: You have been a teacher for me. Though our journey together has not always been an easy one, we have never doubted the deep love we share. Many things get in the way of everyday life, but I know in the deepest spaces of my heart that if I needed you, you'd be there. I'm grateful to know that our hearts are always connected. I love you from the bottom of my heart.

To Cathy, my dear childhood friend (since second grade): Thank you for the "kick in the butt" when I needed it, along with your kind words and encouragement. Thank you for standing beside me through the crazy childhood and the glorious adulthood. Thanks for being my college buddy, apartment sharer, and close neighbor. I will always cherish you.

To Pat, my dear friend (over thirty-five years), who has shared her wisdom and experiences with me for many years: You have been a voice of reason and respect. You've always been able to share the world I'm going into with enthusiasm and grace. You have been a role model to me. I thank you for being *you* and sharing your life perspectives. Thank you for taking the time to share it all with me. I will forever be grateful for my Kansas getaways to be with my dear friend. I will always be appreciative and grateful for you. Thanks for helping me grow.

To Debbie, my friend: There are no words for my gratefulness. When I finally crashed and burned (emotionally), you gently held my heart, with both hands, until I could take it back and soar again. Your gifts are precious and rare. I have the greatest respect, admiration, and love for you, my friend. Thank you for your expertise, understanding, and willingness to take me on a journey to once again brighten my soul. You are a light keeper. In a world of chaos, you remind good people to stay strong, no matter how difficult it may seem. Your mission is of goodness. My heart wishes you the same goodness that you so freely give. Much love and light to you always.

To those who have passed on but still give me insight, intuition, and understanding:

My dad, Richard (Dick), for teaching me to respect all things and for giving me curiosity, wonderment, and awe. As you passed on early, I thank you for giving me the greatest coping skill, which guided me through life—the understanding and love of nature.

My mom, Dolores (Dee), for showing me how to be helpful to others, be responsible for myself, and that by putting on a smile, I can truly turn a sad day into a good day. Thank you for always listening, even when we disagreed. I will always hold dear to my heart how you persevered through one difficulty after another, leaving friends and family shaking their heads in amazement. Thank you for showing me how to just "keep moving forward."

My brother Wade, for valuing education and showing me the path. Even though you passed on too early, you left your mark on students, faculty, friends, and family. You were loved by many, laughed with many, and helped so many. Thank you for sharing your love of teaching and coaching. Your passions created many positive ripple effects. Thank you for showing me the love of teaching and education.

Finally, thank you to Dr. Ed (and wife, Betty) Salm, professor of anthropology at Southwestern College in Winfield, Kansas, for letting me live with them for a whole summer before my junior year of college started. I had no place to go, and you took me in. I will be forever grateful and appreciative for your belief in me and the safe place you created, never once asking for anything in return. Your kindness and generosity will never be forgotten. You helped me believe in the goodness of human beings. And to Dr. Barbara Bebensee, professor of counseling psychology at CU Denver, Denver, Colorado, who saw the therapist in me. Thank you for believing in my abilities, my knowledge, and my future. Thank you for becoming my friend, my colleague, and my cheerleader.

Thank you all for helping me every day to be the best person I can be.

ABOUT THE AUTHOR

Cheri Henke Kretsch grew up as a mountain girl in Colorado. Born as a carefree lover of life, the only world she knew was filled with animals, nature and a loving family. After experiencing traumatic events in childhood and adolescence, the mountains taught her, once again, to trust and love. Living in nature gave her the eyes to see healing, the strength to go on and the heart to share. Her love of nature and the metaphors it creates became a life-long gift to help understand the world she lives in.

Cheri Henke Kretsch is a licensed psychotherapist with twenty-seven years of experience working for large companies, on military bases, and in private practice. In addition, Henke Kretsch has spent over twenty years teaching psychology, working with special-needs students, working as a guidance counselor at the high school level, and working as an adjunct professor of psychology at the college level.

Henke Kretsch is the recipient of the Outstanding Young Educator Award for Kansas and was twice awarded Who's Who in Education. She was Counselor of the Year for Jefferson County Schools, Colorado, and won both the Golden and Silver Poets Award in Washington, DC. Cheri Henke Kretsch currently resides in Littleton, Colorado. She can be contacted at her email address: cheri@natural-lessons.com.

Made in the USA
Columbia, SC
04 August 2021